git

What you need to know

James H. Foster

Table of content

git

Chapter 1: Introduction to Git

Welcome to the world of Git! In this chapter, we will explore what Git is, why it's important, and how it can benefit you as a programmer. We will also delve into the Git workflow and guide you through the installation and setup process. By the end of this chapter, you'll have a solid understanding of the fundamentals of Git and be ready to dive deeper into its features and functionalities.

What is Git and why it's important

Git is a distributed version control system that allows you to track changes to your code over time. It was created by Linus Torvalds, the same genius behind Linux, and has become the de facto standard for version control in the software development industry.

Imagine this scenario: you're working on a project with a team of developers, and each of you is making changes to the codebase. Without a version control system like Git, it would be a nightmare to keep track of who made what changes, when they were made, and how they affected the overall codebase. Git solves this problem by providing a centralized repository where all changes are logged, allowing you to easily collaborate with others, roll back changes if necessary, and maintain a clean and organized codebase.

Version control and its benefits

Version control is the management of changes to documents, files, or any set of information. It allows you to track and control different versions of your code, enabling collaboration, reducing the risk of conflicts, and improving the overall quality of your project. Some of the key benefits of version control include:

- Collaboration: With Git, multiple developers can work on the same codebase simultaneously, without stepping on each other's toes. Git keeps track of who made which changes and allows for easy merging of code.

- Reproducibility: Git allows you to recreate any version of your codebase at any point in time. This is particularly useful when troubleshooting bugs or rolling back to a stable version.

- Branching: Git enables you to create separate branches for different features or experiments. This allows you to work on new features without affecting the main codebase, and merge the changes back when they are ready.

-

  Code Reviews: Git makes it easy to review and provide feedback on code changes. By creating pull requests, team members can review, discuss, and suggest improvements before the changes are merged into the main codebase.

Understanding the Git workflow

The Git workflow follows a simple cycle of creating a local copy of a repository, making changes, committing those changes, and then pushing them to a remote repository. This cycle is often referred to as the "clone-commit-push-pull" workflow.

By following this workflow, you can effectively collaborate with others, track changes to your codebase, and ensure that your project remains in a stable and organized state.

Installation and setup of Git

Before you can start using Git, you need to install it on your machine and configure it with your personal information. Here are the steps to get started:

git config --global user.name "Your Name" git config --global user.email "youremail@example.com"

Replace "Your Name" with your actual name and "youremail@example.com" with your email address.

git --version

This should display the version of Git you installed.

With Git successfully installed and configured, you're now ready to start using it for version control and collaboration.

Remember, Git is a powerful tool that can greatly enhance your productivity as a programmer. By understanding its key concepts and mastering its commands, you'll be able to work more efficiently, collaborate seamlessly with others, and have the peace of mind that your code is safely version-controlled. So let's dive in and explore the basic Git commands in the next chapter!

Chapter 2: Basic Git Commands

In this chapter, we will explore the basic Git commands that every programmer should know. These commands are the core of Git and will allow you to navigate, make changes, and collaborate effectively with others. Whether you are a beginner or already familiar with Git, this chapter will provide you with a solid foundation to build upon.

Clone: Creating a local copy of a repository

One of the first steps in working with Git is to clone a repository. Cloning creates a local copy of a remote repository, allowing you to work on the code and contribute changes. To clone a repository, you can use the following command:

git clone <repository-url>

For example, if you want to clone a repository named "my-project" from GitHub, you would use the command:

git   clone   https://github.com/username/my-
project.git

Cloning a repository not only allows you to have a local copy of the code but also sets up a connection between your local copy and the remote repository. This connection enables you to synchronize your changes with the remote repository using other Git commands like commit, push, and pull.

Commit: Saving changes to the repository

Once you have made changes to your code, the next step is to save those changes to the repository. This is where the commit command comes into play. A commit is like taking a snapshot of your changes and creating a new version of the code.

To make a commit, you need to stage the changes first using the git add command. This command allows you to select which changes you want to include in the commit. Once you have staged your changes, you can use the following command to make a commit:

git commit -m "Commit message"

It's important to write clear and descriptive commit messages that explain the purpose of the changes. This will make it easier for others to understand your code and track the progress of the project.

Push: Uploading local changes to a remote repository

After making a commit, your changes are still only saved locally. To share your changes with others and update the remote repository, you need to use the push command. This command uploads your local commits to the remote repository, making them accessible to others.

To push your changes, you can use the following command:

git push

By default, this command pushes the changes to the branch you are currently on. If you want to push to a different branch, you can specify the branch name:

git push origin <branch-name>

It's important to note that you can only push to a branch if you have the necessary permissions. If you are contributing to an open-source project, you might need to create a fork of the repository and push your changes to your fork before creating a pull request.

Pull: Updating the local copy with remote changes

In a collaborative environment, it's common for multiple people to be working on the same codebase. To keep your local copy up to date with the latest changes from the remote repository, you need to use the pull command.

The pull command combines two operations: fetching the latest changes from the remote repository and merging them into your local branch. This ensures that your local copy reflects the current state of the project.

To pull the latest changes from the remote repository, you can use the following command:

git pull

By default, this command pulls the changes from the branch you are currently on. If you want to pull from a different branch, you can specify the branch name:

git pull origin <branch-name>

It's important to pull regularly to avoid conflicts with other people's changes. Conflicts occur when Git is unable to automatically merge the changes and requires manual intervention. We will explore how to resolve merge conflicts in more detail in Chapter 3.

In the next chapter, we will dive into the world of branching and merging, exploring how to work on multiple code paths simultaneously and bring them together seamlessly. Stay tuned and keep coding!

Chapter 3: Branching and Merging

In this chapter, we will dive into the powerful features of branching and merging in Git. These features allow developers to work on multiple versions of a project simultaneously and merge them back together seamlessly. We will explore how to create branches, switch between them, and merge changes successfully. Along the way, we will also discuss how to handle merge conflicts and resolve them effectively.

Creating branches for parallel development

Branching is one of the most fundamental concepts in Git. It allows developers to create separate "branches" of the codebase, enabling parallel development. Each branch represents a different line of development, allowing multiple features or bug fixes to be worked on simultaneously without interfering with each other.

Imagine you are working on a project that requires the development of a new feature while also addressing some critical bugs. By creating separate branches for each task, you can work on them independently without worrying about conflicts. Once the feature or bug fix is completed, it can be merged back into the main branch, combining all the changes seamlessly.

To create a new branch in Git, you can use the command git branch <branch_name>. For example, if you want to create a branch called "feature-xyz", you would run git branch feature-xyz. This creates a new branch, but you are still on the original branch. To switch to the new branch, you can use the command git checkout <branch_name>. So, to switch to the "feature-xyz" branch, you would run git checkout feature-xyz.

Merge: Combining branches together

Once you have completed the development on a branch, it's time to merge it back into the main branch or any other branch you want to integrate it with. The git merge command is used to combine changes from one branch into another.

Let's say you have finished working on the "feature-xyz" branch and want to merge it into the main branch. First, make sure you are on the branch you want to merge the changes into, in this case, the main branch. Then, run the command git merge <branch_name>. So, to merge the "feature-xyz" branch into the main branch, you would run git merge feature-xyz.

Git will automatically merge the changes if there are no conflicts. However, if there are conflicting changes in both branches, Git will pause the merge process and ask you to resolve the conflicts manually. This brings us to the next topic.

Resolving merge conflicts

Merge conflicts occur when Git detects conflicting changes in different branches that cannot be merged automatically. This usually happens when two or more developers modify the same file or the same lines of code independently.

When a merge conflict occurs, Git will mark the conflicting lines in the affected file(s) and insert both versions of the conflicting code. It's then up to the developer to manually resolve the conflict by editing the file and choosing which version of the code to keep.

To resolve merge conflicts, open the conflicting file(s) in a text editor and look for the conflict markers that Git has inserted. These markers typically look like <<<<<<< HEAD, =======, and >>>>>>> <branch_name>. Between the markers, you will see the conflicting code from both branches.

Carefully review the conflicting code and decide which version to keep. Remove the conflict markers and any unnecessary code, leaving only the desired changes. Once you have resolved all conflicts in the file(s), save the changes and run git add <file_name> to mark the conflicts as resolved. Finally, run git commit to complete the merge.

Switching between branches

Git makes it easy to switch between branches, allowing developers to work on different features or bug fixes without any hassle. The git checkout command is used to switch between branches.

To switch to a different branch, simply run git checkout <branch_name>. For example, if you want to switch to the "feature-xyz" branch, you would run git checkout feature-xyz.

It's important to note that any uncommitted changes in your current branch will be carried over when you switch branches. Git will attempt to merge these changes into the new branch automatically. However, if conflicts arise during the merge, you will have to resolve them manually.

Switching between branches is an essential skill in Git, allowing developers to context-switch between different tasks quickly. It promotes a flexible and efficient development workflow, especially when working on multiple features simultaneously.

In the next chapter, we will explore the collaborative features of Git using GitHub, where multiple developers can work together on a project seamlessly. But before that, let's take a moment to appreciate the power of branching and merging in Git. With these features, developers can work on projects with confidence, knowing that changes can be managed and integrated smoothly. So, branch out and merge your way to success in your Git journey!

Chapter 4: Collaboration with GitHub

In this chapter, we will explore how to collaborate with other developers using GitHub. GitHub is a web-based platform that allows for easy sharing and collaboration on projects. It provides a range of features that facilitate teamwork and make working on projects with others a breeze. Whether you are part of a small team or contributing to open-source projects, GitHub has got you covered.

Introduction to GitHub and its features

GitHub is not just a code hosting platform, it is a collaborative platform that brings developers together. It allows for easy sharing, reviewing, and tracking of code changes. GitHub provides a range of features that enhance collaboration and streamline the development process.

One of the key features of GitHub is its repository management. Repositories are like folders that contain all the files and code for a project. With GitHub, you can easily create and manage repositories, making it simple to organize and keep track of your projects.

Repositories: Creating and managing projects

Creating a repository on GitHub is as easy as a few clicks. You can create a new repository directly on the GitHub website, or you can use Git commands to initialize a repository locally and then push it to GitHub. Once a repository is created, you can add files, make changes, and commit those changes to the repository.

GitHub also provides tools to manage your repository. You can track the history of your project with the help of commits, branches, and tags. Commits are like snapshots of your project at a specific point in time, while branches allow for parallel development. Tags are used to mark specific versions of your project.

Issues: Tracking and resolving problems

Issues are a powerful feature of GitHub that allows you to track and resolve problems in your projects. Issues can be used to report bugs, suggest new features, or discuss ideas. When an issue is created, it becomes a central place for discussion and collaboration among team members.

GitHub provides a range of tools to manage issues. You can assign issues to specific team members, add labels to categorize them, and create milestones to track progress. You can also use issue templates to provide guidelines for issue creation, making it easier for team members to report problems effectively.

Pull Requests: Requesting and reviewing code changes

Pull requests are a core feature of GitHub that enables collaboration and code review. When you want to contribute to a project, you can create a pull request to propose changes to the project's codebase. Pull requests provide a way for developers to discuss, review, and refine code changes before merging them into the main project.

GitHub provides a range of tools to facilitate code review. Reviewers can leave comments on specific lines of code, suggest changes, and approve or request changes to the code. Pull requests can also be linked to issues, making it easier to track the progress of code changes and resolve any problems that arise.

Collaborating with others on GitHub can greatly enhance the development process. It allows for easy sharing and tracking of code changes, effective problem tracking and resolution, and streamlined code review. By leveraging the features provided by GitHub, you can work seamlessly with others and create amazing projects together. So, let's dive in and explore the world of collaboration with GitHub!

Chapter 5: GitHub Workflows

In this chapter, we will explore how to effectively collaborate with others using GitHub. GitHub provides a powerful platform for managing projects, tracking issues, and reviewing code changes. By understanding the various workflows available on GitHub, you can enhance your collaboration skills and contribute to open-source projects with confidence.

Forking repositories for personal contributions

One of the key features of GitHub is the ability to fork repositories. Forking allows you to create a personal copy of a repository, which you can modify and make changes to without affecting the original project. This is especially useful when you want to contribute to an open-source project.

When forking a repository, you create a new copy under your GitHub account. You can then clone this forked repository to your local machine and make changes as needed. Once you are satisfied with your changes, you can create a pull request to propose your changes to the original project.

Forking repositories not only allows you to contribute to existing projects, but it also gives you the freedom to experiment and make changes without worrying about breaking anything.

Making changes locally and pushing to GitHub

Once you have forked a repository and cloned it to your local machine, you can start making changes to the code. This can include fixing bugs, adding new features, or improving existing functionality.

To make changes locally, you can use your favorite code editor to modify the files in the repository. Once you are done making changes, it's time to commit and push your changes to GitHub.

Committing changes in Git is like taking a snapshot of your code at a specific point in time. Each commit represents a logical unit of work and should be accompanied by a descriptive commit message. This helps others understand the purpose of your changes and makes it easier to track the history of the project.

To push your changes to GitHub, you can use the git push command. This sends your local commits to your forked repository on GitHub. From there, you can create a pull request to propose your changes to the original project.

Reviewing code and providing feedback

Code reviews are an essential part of the development process. They help ensure that the code meets high-quality standards and that potential issues are identified and resolved early on.

GitHub provides a powerful code review system that allows collaborators to provide feedback on proposed changes. When you create a pull request, others can review your code, leave comments, and suggest modifications. This collaborative approach ensures that the code is thoroughly examined and improved before it is merged into the main project.

When reviewing code, it's important to provide constructive feedback and be respectful of the author's work. Focus on the code's functionality, readability, and adherence to coding standards. By providing clear and actionable feedback, you can help improve the quality of the code and contribute to a positive and collaborative environment.

Merging pull requests and resolving conflicts

Once a pull request has undergone code review and received approval, it can be merged into the main project. GitHub provides several options for merging pull requests, including merging directly, squashing commits, or rebasing.

Merging pull requests can sometimes lead to conflicts if the changes made in the pull request conflict with changes made in the main project. Resolving these conflicts requires careful consideration and collaboration between the parties involved.

GitHub provides a user-friendly interface for resolving conflicts. You can review the conflicting files, make the necessary changes, and commit the resolved files. Once the conflicts are resolved, the pull request can be merged successfully.

Resolving conflicts is an opportunity to engage in constructive discussions and find the best possible solution. By communicating openly and working together, conflicts can be resolved in a way that benefits the project and maintains a positive collaborative atmosphere.

Remember, collaboration is key when working with others on GitHub. Embrace the opportunity to learn from each other, share knowledge, and contribute to the success of the project. With the right mindset and effective communication, GitHub can become a powerful tool for collaboration and open-source contributions.

Conclusion

In this chapter, we explored the various workflows available on GitHub to enhance collaboration and contribute to open-source projects. We learned about forking repositories, making changes locally, and pushing them to GitHub. We also discussed the importance of code reviews and how to provide constructive feedback. Finally, we delved into the process of merging pull requests and resolving conflicts.

By leveraging the features provided by GitHub, you can become an active and valued member of the software development community. Remember to always approach collaboration with an open mind, respect for others' work, and a willingness to learn and grow. Happy collaborating!

Chapter 6: README and Wiki

In this chapter, we will explore the importance of creating a helpful README file and utilizing the Wiki feature on GitHub. These tools not only provide a means of documenting your projects but also serve as a valuable communication platform for collaboration with others.

Creating a helpful README file

A README file is often the first thing that users see when they visit your project repository. It serves as a guide to help them understand what your project is about, how to set it up, and how to contribute. Writing a clear and descriptive README can make a significant difference in attracting users and contributors to your project.

When creating a README, consider including the following information:

Project Description

Start by providing a brief overview of your project. Explain its purpose, its main features, and the problem it solves. Use simple language and avoid technical jargon to ensure that readers can easily understand what your project is about.

Installation Instructions

Include step-by-step instructions on how to install and set up your project. Be sure to specify any dependencies or requirements, and provide code snippets or terminal commands to guide users through the process. If possible, include screenshots to visually demonstrate the installation steps.

Usage and Examples

Explain how users can interact with your project. Provide clear instructions on how to run the project, how to use its main features, and any available command-line options. Include code examples and sample input/output to help users understand how your project works.

Contributing Guidelines

Encourage users to contribute to your project by providing guidelines on how they can get involved. Explain the process for submitting bug reports, feature requests, or code contributions. Include information on how to set up a development environment, how to run tests, and any coding conventions or style guidelines that contributors should follow.

License Information

Specify the license under which your project is released. This is important as it defines the permissions and restrictions for using your code. Choose a license that aligns with your project goals and be sure to include the license file in your repository.

Documenting projects with a Wiki

The Wiki feature on GitHub provides a collaborative platform for documenting your project. It allows users to contribute to the documentation, making it a valuable resource for sharing knowledge and keeping information up to date.

Creating Wiki Pages

To create a Wiki page, navigate to the "Wiki" tab in your repository and click on "New page". Give your page a meaningful title and start adding content using Markdown syntax. You can include headings, lists, images, code snippets, and more to organize and format your content.

Collaborative Editing

One of the great advantages of using the Wiki feature is its collaborative nature. Multiple users can contribute to the documentation by making edits or adding new content. GitHub keeps track of all changes, making it easy to review and revert edits if needed.

Utilizing README and Wiki for project communication

The README file and the Wiki can serve as a means of communication between project maintainers and users. You can use these platforms to announce important updates, share project roadmaps, and address frequently asked questions. By keeping these documents up to date and actively engaging with users, you can build a strong and supportive community around your project.

Remember, a well-documented project is more likely to attract users and contributors. Take the time to create a helpful README file and maintain an informative Wiki. Your efforts will pay off in the long run, as they will contribute to the success and growth of your project.

Chapter 7: Best Practices for Git

In this chapter, we will explore some best practices for using Git effectively and efficiently. By following these guidelines, you can ensure that your codebase remains organized, your collaboration with team members is smooth, and your overall workflow is optimized.

Writing clear and descriptive commit messages

One of the most important aspects of using Git is writing clear and descriptive commit messages. A commit message should succinctly summarize the changes made in the commit and provide enough context for others (including your future self) to understand the purpose and impact of the changes.

Consider the following commit message: "Fixed bug." This message provides no information about what bug was fixed or how it was fixed. Now compare it to this message: "Fixed issue #123: NullPointerException in User class." This message clearly identifies the issue being addressed and provides additional context about the specific problem and solution.

By writing clear and descriptive commit messages, you can easily track and understand changes made to your codebase, making it easier to identify and fix issues, collaborate with team members, and maintain a clean and organized Git history.

Keeping branches focused and organized

When working on a project with multiple branches, it is important to keep your branches focused and organized. Each branch should have a specific purpose and should only contain changes related to that purpose. This helps to avoid confusion, reduce conflicts, and makes it easier to review and merge changes.

Imagine a scenario where you have a single branch that contains several unrelated changes. When it comes time to review and merge the branch, it can be difficult to understand the purpose of each change and ensure that they do not conflict with each other. By keeping branches focused and organized, you can avoid this situation and make the review and merge process much smoother.

If you find yourself making unrelated changes, consider creating separate branches for each change or using Git's stash feature to temporarily save changes while you work on a different task. This will help you keep your branches focused and organized, making collaboration and code review much easier.

Submitting small and atomic pull requests

When collaborating with others using Git, it is important to submit small and atomic pull requests. A pull request should contain a single cohesive set of changes that can be easily reviewed and merged.

Large pull requests that contain a mix of unrelated changes can be overwhelming for reviewers and may result in longer review times and more conflicts. By breaking your work into smaller, more focused pull requests, you can make the review process more efficient and increase the likelihood of your changes being merged quickly.

Additionally, atomic pull requests allow for easier identification and resolution of conflicts. If a conflict arises during the review process, it is much easier to isolate and resolve conflicts in a small, focused pull request compared to a large, complex one.

Effective code reviews and feedback

Code reviews are a crucial part of the development process and can greatly improve the quality of your code. When reviewing code, it is important to provide constructive feedback that helps the author understand any issues or areas for improvement.

Instead of simply pointing out problems, try to offer suggestions or alternative solutions. This will not only help the author address the issue but also encourage their growth and learning. Remember, the goal of a code review is to improve the code and the skills of the author, not to criticize or belittle their work.

When receiving code reviews, it is important to approach feedback with an open mind. Remember that code reviews are an opportunity for growth and improvement, and that feedback is not a personal attack. Take the time to understand the feedback and ask for clarification if needed. By approaching code reviews with a positive and open mindset, you can learn from others and become a better developer.

By following these best practices for Git, you can enhance your workflow, improve collaboration with team members, and maintain a clean and organized codebase. Remember to write clear and descriptive commit messages, keep your branches focused and organized, submit small and atomic pull requests, and provide effective code reviews and feedback. Following these guidelines will not only make your Git experience more enjoyable but also lead to better code and more successful projects.

Chapter 8: Troubleshooting Git

Git is a powerful tool for version control, but like any tool, it can sometimes be a bit tricky to work with. In this chapter, we'll explore some common issues that you might encounter while using Git and how to troubleshoot them effectively. From resolving merge conflicts to dealing with detached heads, we'll cover it all. So, let's dive in!

Understanding merge conflicts and resolving them

Merge conflicts can occur when Git is unable to automatically merge changes from different branches. This usually happens when two or more branches have made conflicting changes to the same file. When a merge conflict occurs, Git will mark the conflicting sections in the file and it's your job to resolve them.

Resolving merge conflicts can be a bit daunting, but fear not! Here are some steps to help you navigate through the process:

Remember, communication is key when resolving merge conflicts. Reach out to your teammates to understand their changes and collaborate on finding the best solution. It's always better to have a discussion and reach a consensus rather than forcefully imposing your changes.

Rebasing vs merging: When to use each

Rebasing and merging are two different ways to integrate changes from one branch into another. Understanding when to use each method is crucial to maintain a clean and organized Git history.

Merging is the default method in Git and is suitable for most scenarios. It creates a new commit that combines the changes from both branches. Merging is useful when you want to preserve the history of both branches and maintain a clear separation between them.

Rebasing, on the other hand, allows you to apply the changes from one branch on top of another branch. It essentially moves the entire branch to a new base commit. Rebasing can help create a linear history, making it easier to follow the progression of changes.

So, when should you use each method? Here's a general rule of thumb:

- Use merging when you want to integrate changes from a feature branch into a main branch, such as merging a feature branch into a develop branch.

- Use rebasing when you want to incorporate the latest changes from a main branch into a feature branch, such as rebasing a feature branch onto the latest commits in the develop branch.

Remember, both methods have their pros and cons, so choose the one that best suits your workflow and project requirements.

Dealing with detached heads

A detached head state in Git occurs when you checkout a commit instead of a branch. In this state, any new commits you make won't be attached to a branch, making them difficult to access later.

Detached heads can happen accidentally, but they can also be useful in certain scenarios, such as when you need to inspect an old commit or create a new branch based on a specific commit. However, if you find yourself in a detached head state unintentionally, here's how you can get back on track:

By following these steps, you can easily recover from a detached head state and continue working on your project without any hiccups.

Resetting the repository to a previous state

Sometimes, you might find yourself in a situation where you want to undo some or all of the changes in your Git repository and get back to a previous state. Git provides the reset command to help you achieve this.

The git reset command allows you to move the current branch pointer to a specified commit, effectively resetting the repository to that commit. There are three types of reset: --soft, --mixed, and --hard.

- --soft reset moves the branch pointer to the specified commit but leaves the changes in the working directory and staging area. This can be useful when you want to undo the last commit but keep the changes for further modifications.

- --mixed reset is the default mode and moves the branch pointer to the specified commit while also clearing the staging area. This effectively "unstages" the changes but keeps them in the working directory. This mode is handy when you want to undo the last commit and discard its changes.

-
  --hard reset moves the branch pointer to the specified commit, clears the staging area, and discards all changes in the working directory. This mode is more destructive and should be used with caution as it permanently removes any uncommitted changes.

Remember, resetting the repository can be a powerful tool, but it's important to use it wisely. Always make sure to create a backup or branch off before performing any reset operations to avoid losing any important work.

And that wraps up our troubleshooting journey in Git! By understanding how to resolve merge conflicts, when to use rebasing or merging, how to deal with detached heads, and how to reset the repository to a previous state, you'll be well-equipped to tackle any challenges that come your way. So, keep calm and Git on!

Chapter 9: Git Configuration

In this chapter, we will explore the different aspects of Git configuration and how it can enhance your workflow. Git configuration allows you to customize various settings and personalize your Git experience. By sctting up user information, creating aliases, and customizing Git commands, you can make your Git usage more efficient and tailored to your needs.

Setting up user information in Git

When you start using Git, it's important to configure your user information so that your commits are properly attributed. This information includes your name and email address, which will be associated with each commit you make. To set up your user information, you can use the following commands:

```bash
git config --global user.name "Your Name"
git config --global user.email "your@email.com"
```

By using the --global flag, you can set this information globally for all your Git repositories. If you want to set it only for a specific repository, you can omit the --global flag.

Setting up your user information is not only important for proper attribution but also helps in identifying your contributions when collaborating with others. It's a good practice to use a consistent and recognizable name and email address across your projects.

Creating aliases for frequently used commands

Git commands can sometimes be long and cumbersome to type. To make your workflow more efficient, you can create aliases for frequently used commands. Aliases are shortcuts that you can define for Git commands, allowing you to use shorter and more memorable names.

For example, instead of typing git status every time you want to check the status of your repository, you can create an alias like git st. To create an alias, you can use the git config command with the --global flag:

bash
git config --global alias.st status

Now, you can simply type git st to get the status of your repository. You can create aliases for any

Git command, and even chain multiple commands together to create more complex aliases.

Creating aliases can greatly speed up your workflow and make your commands easier to remember. It's worth taking the time to set up aliases for the commands you use frequently.

Customizing Git commands

In addition to creating aliases, you can also customize the behavior of Git commands by modifying the Git configuration. This allows you to tailor Git to your specific needs and preferences.

For example, you can change the default text editor used by Git to your preferred editor. By default, Git uses the system's default editor, but you can change it by setting the core.editor configuration:

bash
git config --global core.editor "nano"

Now, whenever you need to enter a commit message or edit a file in Git, it will open in the nano editor.

You can also customize other aspects of Git, such as the colors used in the output, the default branch name, and the behavior of various commands. The possibilities are endless, and you can experiment with different configurations to find what works best for you.

Enhancing the Git workflow with configuration

Git configuration allows you to go beyond the default settings and tailor Git to your specific needs. By setting up user information, creating aliases, and customizing Git commands, you can enhance your Git workflow and make it more efficient.

However, it's important to strike a balance between customization and consistency. While it's great to personalize Git to suit your preferences, it's also important to follow best practices and conventions to ensure compatibility and collaboration with others.

In the next chapter, we will explore common Git workflows that you can adopt depending on your project and team structure. Stay tuned to discover the best workflow for your needs!

Chapter 10: Common Git Workflows

In this chapter, we will explore some of the most common Git workflows that developers use in different scenarios. Whether you are working alone on a project, collaborating with a team, contributing to open-source projects, or managing software versions, there is a Git workflow that suits your needs. We will dive into each workflow and provide practical steps, tips, and best practices to help you navigate through your projects smoothly.

Individual Workflow: Working Alone on a Project

Working alone on a project can be both liberating and challenging. Without the need to coordinate with others, you have the freedom to experiment and make changes at your own pace. However, it is important to maintain good version control practices to ensure the stability and maintainability of your project.

When working individually, it is recommended to follow these steps:

Collaborative Workflow: Working in a Team

Working in a team requires effective coordination and collaboration. Git provides several features and workflows that facilitate teamwork and ensure a smooth development process. Here are the steps to follow when working collaboratively:

Forking Workflow: Contributing to Open-Source Projects

Contributing to open-source projects is a great way to learn from experienced developers and give back to the community. Git provides a forking workflow that enables you to make contributions to a project without directly modifying the original repository. Here is how the forking workflow works:

Release Workflow: Managing Software Versions

Managing software versions is crucial for ensuring stability and delivering new features to users. Git provides several mechanisms to manage software versions, including tags and branches. Here is how you can use Git to manage software versions effectively:

Remember, these are just some of the common Git workflows, and there are many variations and combinations that can be tailored to your specific needs. Experiment with different workflows and find the one that works best for you and your team. Happy coding!

Chapter 11: Git Tips and Tricks

Welcome to Chapter 11 of our book on Git! In this chapter, we'll dive into some handy tips and tricks that will help you become a Git power user. These tips will not only make your workflow more efficient but also save you time and headaches. So, let's get started!

Managing large files with Git LFS

Have you ever tried to commit a large file to your Git repository, only to be met with an error message about the file size limit? We've all been there. Thankfully, Git provides a solution called Git Large File Storage (LFS). Git LFS allows you to store large files outside of your repository, while still keeping track of them using Git.

Let's say you're working on a project that involves large media files, such as images or videos. Instead of bloating your repository with these files, you can use Git LFS to store them elsewhere. This not only keeps your repository lean and fast but also allows you to collaborate on these files with your team.

To get started with Git LFS, you'll need to install it on your system and initialize it in your repository. Once that's done, you can start tracking large files using the git lfs track command. Git LFS will automatically replace these files with pointers in your repository, making it lightweight and manageable.

Using Git hooks for automation

As a developer, you're probably familiar with repetitive tasks that you have to perform every day, such as running tests, formatting code, or deploying changes. Git hooks can come to your rescue by automating these tasks whenever certain Git events occur.

Git hooks are scripts that Git executes before or after events such as committing, pushing, or merging. They allow you to perform custom actions, such as running a script or triggering a build, to streamline your workflow. This not only saves you time and effort but also ensures consistency and reduces the chances of human error.

For example, let's say you want to run your test suite every time you commit changes to your repository. You can create a pre-commit hook that runs your tests and prevents the commit if any of them fail. This way, you can catch issues early on and ensure that your codebase remains stable.

Undoing changes in Git

We've all made mistakes while working with Git. Whether it's committing a wrong file, making unwanted changes, or accidentally deleting something important, Git provides several ways to undo these mistakes and restore your repository to a previous state.

One of the most common ways to undo changes in Git is by using the git reset command. This command allows you to move the HEAD pointer and the current branch pointer to a previous commit, effectively discarding any changes made after that commit. However, be cautious when using git reset as it can be a destructive operation, especially if you force push the changes to a remote repository.

Another way to undo changes is by using the git revert command. Unlike git reset, git revert creates a new commit that undoes the changes made in a previous commit. This is a safer approach as it doesn't alter the commit history, making it more suitable for collaborative projects.

Optimizing Git performance

As your Git repository grows, you may start to notice a decrease in performance. Slow commands, long history, and large files can all contribute to this. However, there are several steps you can take to optimize Git's performance and ensure a smooth experience.

One of the first things you can do is to enable Git's delta compression algorithm, which reduces the size of your repository by storing only the differences between files. This can significantly improve Git's performance, especially when dealing with large files or frequent commits.

Another optimization technique is to periodically run Git's garbage collection (git gc) command. Garbage collection cleans up unnecessary files and optimizes the storage of your repository. By running this command regularly, you can keep your repository lean and fast.

Additionally, you can use Git's shallow clone feature to fetch only a limited depth of commits, instead of the entire history. This can be useful when you only need the latest snapshot of a repository and don't care about its entire history.

Conclusion

In this chapter, we explored some valuable tips and tricks to enhance your Git workflow. From managing large files with Git LFS to automating tasks with Git hooks, and from undoing changes to optimizing Git's performance, these tips will make you a Git power user.

Remember, Git is a powerful tool with countless possibilities. Don't be afraid to experiment, try out different workflows, and discover what works best for you. The more you use Git, the more proficient you'll become. So, keep learning, keep exploring, and keep pushing your boundaries.

In the next chapter, we'll review the key concepts of Git, summarize what we've learned so far, and provide additional resources and further reading. Stay tuned!

Chapter 12: Wrap-up and Next Steps

Congratulations! You've made it to the final chapter of this book. By now, you should have a solid understanding of Git and its various features. You've learned about version control, the Git workflow, and how to perform basic commands like clone, commit, push, and pull. You've also delved into more advanced topics such as branching, merging, collaboration with GitHub, and troubleshooting common issues.

In this chapter, we'll review the key concepts of Git, explore some advanced features, and provide you with additional resources and next steps to continue your journey as a Git expert.

Reviewing the Key Concepts of Git

Before we dive into advanced Git features, let's take a moment to review the key concepts you've learned throughout this book. Git is a distributed version control system that allows multiple developers to work on a project simultaneously. It tracks changes made to files and folders, allowing you to easily revert to previous versions if needed. The three main states of a file in Git are untracked, staged, and committed.

You've also learned about the importance of clear and descriptive commit messages, keeping branches focused and organized, and submitting small and atomic pull requests. These best practices help maintain a clean and efficient Git workflow.

Advancing Your Git Skills and Knowledge

Now that you have a solid foundation in Git, it's time to take your skills to the next level. There are several advanced features and techniques you can explore to further enhance your Git workflow.

Git Hooks for Automation

Git hooks are scripts that can be triggered at certain points in the Git workflow. They allow you to automate tasks such as running tests, formatting code, or sending notifications. By leveraging Git hooks, you can save time and ensure that your codebase meets certain quality standards.

For example, you can set up a pre-commit hook that automatically runs unit tests before each commit. This ensures that your code is always in a working state and reduces the chances of introducing bugs.

Undoing Changes in Git

Mistakes happen, and Git provides several ways to undo changes. The git revert command allows you to create a new commit that undoes the changes made in a previous commit. This is useful when you want to keep a record of the mistake and its resolution.

On the other hand, the git reset command allows you to move the current branch pointer to a previous commit, effectively discarding any commits that come after it. This should be used with caution, as it can permanently remove commits from your repository.

Optimizing Git Performance

As your project grows, you might start to notice that Git's performance decreases. Large repositories with many files and commits can become slow to work with. Fortunately, there are several strategies you can employ to optimize Git's performance.

One approach is to use the Git LFS (Large File Storage) extension for managing large files. Git LFS replaces large files with text pointers, reducing the size of your repository. This makes cloning and fetching faster, as only the pointers are transferred.

Another strategy is to use shallow cloning, which allows you to fetch only a subset of the commit history. This can significantly reduce the time it takes to clone a repository, especially if you're only interested in the latest commits.

Additional Resources and Further Reading

Git is a powerful tool with a wealth of features and possibilities. This book has provided you with a solid foundation, but there is always more to learn. Here are some additional resources and further reading to continue your Git journey:

-
  Pro Git by Scott Chacon and Ben Straub: This book is the definitive guide to Git. It covers everything from the basics to advanced topics and is available for free online.

-
  Git Documentation: The official Git documentation is a comprehensive resource that covers all aspects of Git. It includes tutorials, reference guides, and troubleshooting tips.

-
  GitHub Guides: GitHub provides a collection of guides that cover various aspects of Git and GitHub. These guides are well-written and include practical examples.

- Stack Overflow: Stack Overflow is a popular Q&A platform where developers can ask questions and get answers from the community. It's a great resource for troubleshooting Git issues and finding solutions to common problems.

Remember, becoming an expert in Git takes time and practice. Don't be afraid to experiment, make mistakes, and learn from them. The more you use Git, the more comfortable and proficient you will become.

Conclusion

In this book, we've covered the fundamentals of Git, explored advanced features, and provided tips and best practices to help you become a Git expert. We hope that you've found this book informative and engaging.

Remember, Git is a powerful tool that can greatly improve your development workflow. Embrace it, experiment with it, and use it to collaborate with others. With Git, you have the power to track changes, collaborate effectively, and confidently manage your projects.

Thank you for joining us on this journey through Git. We hope that you continue to explore and discover the endless possibilities that Git has to offer. Happy coding!

www.ingramcontent.com/pod-product-compliance
Lightning Source LLC
Chambersburg PA
CBHW050746260726
48661CB00001B/446